Let's Start
a Scrapbook
for Girls

Scrap attack

Written by Lisa Regan
Scrapbook layouts designed by Sigrid Schroeder
Layout by custardfish

TOP THAT! Kids™

Published by Top That! Publishing plc
Tide Mill Way, Woodbridge, Suffolk, IP12 1AP, UK
www.topthatpublishing.com
Top That! Kids is a Trademark of Top That! Publishing plc
0 2 4 6 8 9 7 5 3 1
Printed and bound in China

Let's Start a Scrapbook for Girls

Let's Start Scrapbooking!

Scrapbooking is a great hobby for everyone. No matter how 'arty' you are, you can still create fabulous pages full of your own memories and experiences – a keepsake for you.

How It Works

This book is split into two sections; techniques and projects. The first section contains loads of useful info about techniques used by professionals so have a read before 'attacking' the projects! Once you've decided it's time to start a project, you'll find lots of cross references to the relevant techniques pages in the first section.

Buying a Scrapbook

Scrapbooking albums can be bought from craft shops in a massive range of shapes and sizes. The projects in this book have all been produced on squares measuring 21 cm x 21 cm, but buy whichever size best fits your layout. Scrapbooks don't have to be expensive – there are plenty of traditional scrapbooks out there filled with sugar paper sheets that will work well.

4

Prepare with Care

Lots of people create scrapbooks as family heirlooms, to be kept for many years. If you plan to do this, you need to be careful in the preparation of your pages. Photos can be spoilt by other items touching them. Certain papers and pens, for example, contain acids which gradually ruin your scrapbook pages. If you don't want this to happen, always buy specialist scrapbooking pens and paper which are marked 'acid free'.

However, you might not be too worried about keeping your efforts to pass on to your children! Just make sure you're not using the only precious copy of something that can't be replaced, such as a special birthday photo, and you'll be fine.

Laying out a Page

To create a finished page, you'll need to experiment with different arrangements, or layouts, using a selection of photos and extra items. Don't stick anything down until you're really sure where everything needs to be.

Which Memory?

Begin by choosing a theme for a page. You might want to keep memories of the day you were a bridesmaid, or had a birthday party, or received your first Valentine's card. Sort through all the photos of that event and choose the best ones. Put them with the special things that go with them – a ribbon from your bouquet, or a copy of your invitations, or the Valentine's card itself.

There isn't a 'right' number of photos you need for one project – it depends on the size of your page and the photos. You might want one large one and a couple of little ones, or four which are all the same size.

6

Draw the Eye

Many scrapbookers divide their page into nine sections, like a noughts and crosses grid. The four points where the lines cross near the middle of the page are the main focus points for your most important items. The grid also splits the page into thirds (either across or down) if you want to feature three items equally.

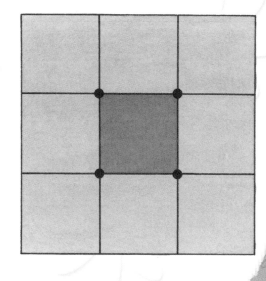

Give it Room!

When you're planning your page, allow extra space around your main photos for framing (see page 27) and matting (see page 16).

Scrapattack Tip

Study magazines and books to see how their pages are designed. Look at old books for ideas if you're making a family album with old-fashioned photos.

Colour and Shapes

Look carefully at the photos you're using on your page.
They will help you to choose the colour scheme for the
whole layout, and you will see what shapes work best.

Colour and Theme

Choose colours that work well with the
theme of your page. Bright colours are
great for parties and happy memories,
such as a day at the beach. Pastel colours
work well with baby photos and
weddings. Natural colours are great for
outdoor snaps.

Bring Out the Colour

Often, the colours of the photo can be picked up in
the background. For example, if your photo is of
someone wearing pink, (as in the photo shown left)
use the same pink in your matting (see
page 16) or as part of the background.

Basic Templates

The shape of your photos and other items on the page is important for the overall look. To make a heart-shaped template, (above), first draw the shape on scrap paper. Cut it out and position the hole over the photo, like a frame. When you're happy that it's the right shape and size to fit the photo properly, draw around the shape using a soft pencil. Cut out the shape carefully with scissors and gently rub out any pencil marks that are left.

Scrapattack Tip
Colour blocking is a simple way to make a bold page. Choose two of the main colours from your picture, and use them in blocks in the background.

Backgrounds

Your background is your blank canvas. The materials you use in it should draw attention to the focal points, but not overpower them. *Use your imagination* – backgrounds don't have to be boring!

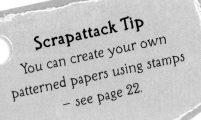

Scrapattack Tip
You can create your own patterned papers using stamps – see page 22.

Be Prepared

If you're buying your background from a craft shop, it's best to select your photos and then take them with you when you choose your patterned papers. That way, you can match colours and themes exactly.

Bringing Out the Detail

Backgrounds can be quite simple, like the colour blocking described on page 9, or more complicated. Lines and shapes can lead your eye to the main photographs. Strips of background paper, borders or ribbons can be used across the pages to guide your eye to the focal points. Great backgrounds use details from the photographs. A ballet photograph, for example, could have pieces of material attached to match your tutu.

Gathering Materials

Collect together as many things as you can to use in your backgrounds. Wrapping paper, foil, scraps of material, tissue paper, wallpaper and even newspaper will all give different effects. Photocopy items that are more bulky and use the copies as backgrounds. Old negatives from cameras make a great backgrounds too, or you could use them as a funky way to matt really tiny photos (see page 16).

Touch 'n' Feel

Look carefully at the textures in your photos. Use these as inspiration for your backgrounds. It's great to run your fingers over a scrapbook page and feel rough sandpaper, smooth silk or bumpy corrugated card.

Paper Effects

Paper is your most important resource!
There are lots of tricks you can play to achieve
some very different and fun effects.

No Scissors Required

Don't use scissors to cut your paper
every time. Try tearing it instead. It
gives different effects on different
papers. Sometimes, it gives you a
white edge which acts as a highlight.
Sometimes, it tears neatly. Other times,
it goes crazy!

Scrapattack Tip
Use a wet cotton bud to draw a
line where you want to tear. This
weakens the fibres in the paper to
make it tear where you want it to.
(This doesn't work on all types of
paper, so experiment!)

Crease It Up

Scrunch up your paper and then smooth it out again. The creases will give you a great effect to use in backgrounds. If you're using very thick paper, spray it with water before you scrunch it. Let it dry completely before sticking it in place.

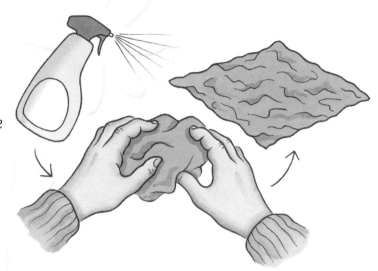

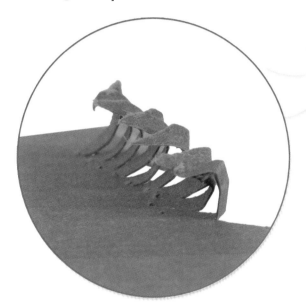

Rolling Your Edges

Try this effect on a torn edge. Make tiny scissor snips into the edge at random intervals. Place the paper on a flat surface, and use your fingers or a pencil to roll the edge. Do it gently, and roll it as tightly or as loosely as you like. It's a great effect to frame a wild picture so it looks like it's bursting out of the page!

Funky and Fluffy

Here's another way to add an edge to your backgrounds if you're using thick card. It gives an old-fashioned feel if it's used on faded colours, or it can look funky if it's used with bright colours and modern designs. Hold your piece of card horizontally. Use a single blade of a pair of scissors to scrape the edge, working away from your body for safety (ask an adult to accompany you while you do this). Continue until the edge is jagged.

Cropping Photos

Your pages will look more like an ordinary photo album than a scrapbook if you don't crop some of your photographs to make them different shapes and sizes. However, don't go mad!

How much to crop?

Do your photos need cropping, or can they stay as they are? Landscape photos, like that of the sea (top left) look best left as they are — but with rounded corners for a neat look. Other photos may have been taken with lots of dull items in the background, so it's best to cut around the focal point in a circle, such as the dog photo (left). Some contain a tiny item of interest — like the rabbit — so cut around it, removing the background completely and use it as page decoration.

Background Clues

Be careful not to crop away background items that are important. If you've devoted a page to your visit to the Eiffel Tower, then there's little point cropping the photo so much that you can't see it! The illustration (right) shows just the right amount to crop.

Join the Dots

Learning to crop neat squares takes a bit of practise. Choose your focal point, then measure an equal distance up, down, left and right of this point and mark each with a dot. Join the dots with a ruler and mark with a soft pencil. This should make only a slight indent in the photo. Then check your lines are straight, and cut just inside your pencil line.

Creative Circles

To crop a circle or oval, get hold of a stencil containing lots of different-sized holes for you to draw around – like the yellow stencil in the photo, shown left. Or, use a pair of compasses to create circles to the exact size you want. To create neat rounded edges, turn your photos over, place a coin in one corner and draw around it. Repeat with the remaining corners, then cut around your curved lines.

Matting

This is probably the most important technique you need to learn before you start creating scrapbook pages. Instead of framing some photos, you can build up layers of paper or card behind them.

Matting Options

You can use a single mat behind a photo, or several layers of matting. As with cropping, less is more. Don't use lots of layers behind every photo on your page. To create a focal point for an important photo, use three layers of matting. Don't forget to alternate between the layers, for example, your second layer could have a decorative edge.

How To Do It!

If you're matting a photo with a straight edge, glue the photo in the corner of your matting paper, with a small amount of paper showing around the edge. Measure the same amount around the other edges and trim to fit, as shown (right).

Bringing It Out

Choose your matting paper carefully to complement the colours of your photograph. In this double matt, lime green paper has been used directly around the photo to highlight it, and the second layer picks out the pink in the girls' clothes. Have fun with shapes, too – these lips match the fun, girly mood of the photo.

Creating Circles and Shapes

If you have cropped a photo into a circle, you'll need a template for your mat. For these basic shapes, simply draw around a household object, such as an old CD or an upturned glass. For more complex shapes, a footprint, for example, invest in a specialist disc set, which will guide your pencil to make a perfect, larger copy.

Scrapattack Tip

You can tear the edges of your matting as on page 12 to make it more interesting.

Using Vellum

Vellum is a type of see-through paper, a bit like tracing paper, but thicker. It's available in different colours and patterns. Look out for it in craft shops.

Toning it Down

Vellum is great for creating different effects on your page. It tones down the colour of anything underneath it, so you can use bright backgrounds but make them duller with vellum on top. It can be used to add a pattern over a background without drastically changing the colour. Vellum on its own also makes for an interesting background, especially if it is printed with a fancy design, such as a map, or patterns, like the papers shown on the left.

Scrapattack Tip
Vellum looks great attached with novel items such as stitching or brads (split pins). See pages 21 and 34 for more about this.

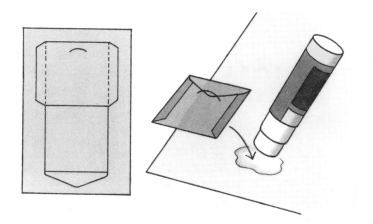

Handy Holder

Vellum pockets can be used to hold items that you want to be visible, but don't want to glue down. To make one, draw a larger version of the outline (left) onto your sheet. Cut it out, and fold along the dotted lines. Stick the sides down, then glue the back to your page.

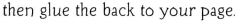

Tricks with Vellum

Vellum can be used like tracing paper to add writing to your scrapbook. Place it over the top of a word that you want to copy. Use a permanent pen to write or draw over the word, and then cut your vellum into shape. Also try tearing it and sticking it down in strips, as seen in the bottom of the project shown to the right.

Get Stuck In!

Always think carefully about how you are going to attach your items to your page. There are lots of different types of adhesives you can use, many of which have special uses.

Choosing your Glue

Photos and paper can be stuck in place with paper glue. Make sure the glue goes all the way to the edge, so the edges don't begin to curl up. If you are gluing material or very thin paper, this kind of glue will show through. Use double-sided tape (bought from craft shops) instead. Spray mount (spray-on glue from a can) is useful for sticking delicate items, but always use it in a well-ventilated area as the fumes are dangerous and unpleasant. Craft glue is good for sticking heavier paper items.

Heavy Items

Some embellishments, such as the yellow buttons on the project shown (right) can be bulky and therefore hard to stick in place. Glue dots – peel-off blobs of glue, or sticky foam pads (see page 25) will hold these items securely.

Get Stitching

Sewing is a great way to hold things in place, and decorate your scrapbook at the same time. A row of running stitch looks fab along the edge of paper or material in the background, or around a photograph as a frame.

Sewing Thicker Card

If your card is too thick to let you pass the needle through easily, use a needle and a ruler to make the holes before you sew. Carefully press the needle along your card at regular intervals, as shown (left). It will be much easier to pass the needle and thread through.

21

Stamping

This is a great way to add decoration to your page. You can repeat a pattern in the background on a single page, or stamp individual characters to cut out.

Paint and Ink

First, get hold of some rubber stamps. If they come with an ink pad, great, but you might want to mix paint to your chosen colour. Roll the stamper across your ink pad, or dab it in your paint, then gently press and release the stamper onto your page. Let the paint dry before you cut the paper and stick it in place. You can buy stamps from craft shops, or you can make your own as shown opposite. Experiment with colours — try using a bright green Christmas tree on a paler green background for contrast, or print one colour over another — moving the second stamp slightly away from the first — for a shadow effect.

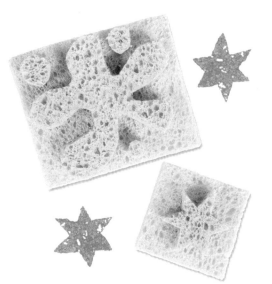

Sponge and Stamp

To make a stamp to your own design, you'll need one sponge block, and a sponge cut into sections. Draw your design onto one of the sections, cut it out and stick it onto the block. Repeat until it's thick enough to print with. If you carefully wash your stamp in warm water afterwards, you can use it again.

Print with a Potato

To make a stamp quickly (but not one that will last very long!) ask an adult to cut a potato in half. Then sketch your shape out in felt-tip, and ask an adult to help you cut away the area around it, leaving a raised shape about 1 cm deep. Blot the starchy potato juice onto kitchen paper before attempting to print with the stamp.

Scrapattack Tip
Remember, whatever your design looks like on the stamp, it will print in reverse when you press it onto paper!

Stickers and Punches

Add extra patterns to your pages by sticking additional items on to form borders or features. These can be stickers, or cut-out shapes made with a punch.

What to Buy?

There's a huge choice of stickers available in the shops nowadays. Some of them are just waiting to be included in your scrapbook! They're a great way to add text without having to do your neatest handwriting. Look for packs of 'best friends' stickers with slogans to use alongside all of your buddies. You can add hearts and flowers to these pages, or to a Valentine's page – look out for super-shimmery stickers in gorgeous colours.

Spelling it Out

Buy packs of alphabet stickers to spell out titles, names and dates of special occasions. Spell out your message on top of the sticker paper first, with half of the letters sticking off the paper. Make sure the spacing is even, and then position the message onto your page. Now press down the top half of the letters, slide away the sticker paper, and smooth the bottom half into place.

Punching Effects

Shop-bought punches cut small, neat motifs from any paper or thin card you choose. Punch out several to decorate your page and stick down randomly for a scattered look. Try overlapping punched shapes of different colours to add contrast.

Using Layers

Experiment with different materials and layers. This 3-D rose has been made from four punched-out circles of tissue paper. The circles were snipped into flower shapes, then a bead threaded through the centre. The rose was then simply scrunched slightly, and the layers 'fluffed up'.

Adding Dimension

Both stickers and punched shapes can be raised off the page with padded sticky pads from craft shops. Cut the mount to fit on the back of your shape, then peel away the two backing papers to fix them in place.

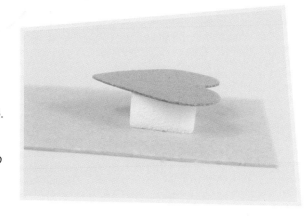

25

Customizing Cut-outs

Shaped card pieces can be bought as die-cuts, which means they're punched into a card sheet so that you can push them out – or you can make your own. Either way, most of the fun is in customizing them!

Make a Cardboard Frame

Cardboard frames are easy to make. Draw your frame onto card and cut around the edge. Then cut the middle bit out. Place your frame over your photo, and wiggle it around until you're happy with the bit of the photo that peeps through. Hold the frame and photo together, then draw around the inner section with a soft pencil. Cut around the pencil mark, leaving a small border. Glue around this border, and stick your photo to the frame.

Scrapattack Tip
If you buy die-cuts, use tweezers to help you push fiddly small parts out of the card else you might tear them.

Creating Shadows

Die-cut letters are very useful for headings and titles. You can either buy a set of alphabet card letters, or make your own – use a stencil to draw the letters you need, then cut them out with sharp scissors. Then use these letters to draw around to make more letters the same. Try using your two sets of letters to spell a word, like 'Birthday'. Glue them so that the second set of letters is underneath the first, with only a fraction showing like a shadow. You can make the shadow set sit slightly to the left or the right (below).

A Touch of Glitz

Add some sparkle to your pages with glittery versions of images found in catalogues and magazines. Cut out the shapes you want, then mount them onto card. Glue over the areas you want to highlight, then shake glitter over the top. Wait until the glue is dry before shaking off the excess glitter.

Using Chalk

Chalk is really versatile – it adds colour and softness and gives an aged look to papers and photos. Scrapbooking chalk is the easiest type to use, but you can get similar results with the normal type.

Simple Chalk Effects

Define the edges of your photos using chalk rubbed on cotton wool for a soft effect, or apply using a cotton bud for sharp edges. Draw simple motifs, like the flowers, hearts, stars and yacht shown on these pages directly onto your paper.

Warming it Up

To make a piece of white paper look less harsh, rub a cotton wool ball covered in pale-coloured chalk over it in circles. Test the paper next to your photo and background to see if you have the subtle effect you want. Always start with a little chalk and build it up gradually to avoid mistakes. If you do make a mistake, you can quickly rub it out with an artist's eraser.

Adding on the Years

To make a photo look aged, try rubbing the edges with sandpaper, and then applying chalk to the sanded areas. You can use two similar colours to give a misty effect, as in the rabbit photo (top). where purple chalk has been layered over blue.

Bright Star

To make a brilliant shape with a soft middle and sharp edges, make a cardboard frame. Press the frame (or use a stencil) firmly onto your chosen paper and dab chalk onto the hole with cotton wool, then remove with care.

Soft Light

For the reverse effect – a neat shape with softly fading edges, make sure you save the middle part of your card frame when cutting it out. Place the card shape onto your page, and hold it down firmly with your finger. Then rub chalk onto a ball of cotton wool, and sweep the ball around the edges of the shape before lifting it away.

29

Journalling

Journalling is the name given by scrapbookers to writing on your pages. You can use it for headings, labels, poems or thoughts about your theme.

Telling Stories

One way of using journalling is to tell the story of your photographs. Imagine you were sitting next to someone and showing them your pages. Instead of talking to them and explaining what's going on, you can write on the page for everyone to read.

Favourite Lines

You can also write quotes and sayings to add an extra element to your photographs. Choose your favourite line from a poem or song, or just write special words on the page, such as SUCCESS next to photos of you on top of a mountain!

Everest

ACHIEVEMENT

beach

PRIDE

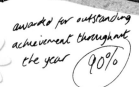

awarded for outstanding achievement throughout the year 90%

SUCCESS

HARD WORK

Writing with Style

There are many different ways of writing your text. If you have neat handwriting, write labels and stick them on to your background. If you prefer, use stencils, stickers or transfers. Ask someone who is good at calligraphy to write out words for you to trace, copy or cut out. There are some great pens in the shops; look for waterproof, fade resistant, acid-free pens with fancy nibs.

Scrapattack Tip
Cut out letters or whole words from magazines and newspapers to create stylish journalling.

Computer Cheat

Here's a great cheat if you're not fond of your own handwriting style. Choose a font on your computer that you like. Type your text and make it the font and the size you want. Change it to a very pale grey and then print it out onto your chosen paper. Write over the top of it so it looks neat, but handwritten!

BOO!

Hand writing

sunny day

School

Magi

STENCIL

Memorabilja

This is the name given to the mementoes that you might want to include in your scrapbook alongside your photographs — they tell the story, and are fun to collect.

Newborn Baby

Make a page for a new birth in the family. Ask your mum if you can take a picture of the hospital bracelet to fix to your page. Use pretty ribbons and baby motifs to decorate the background. If he or she is born with lots of hair, you might even be able to tie a small lock of hair with a ribbon and put it in a vellum pocket!

Scrapattack Tip
Whenever you're out and about, always think about things that you could collect for your scrapbook. The day you score the winning goal in a netball match, for example, shoot a team photo and take home any leaflets associated with the day.

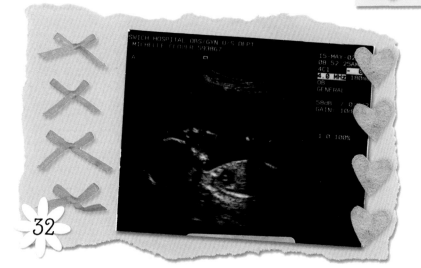

Precious Record

You can include the baby's ultrasound scan picture if you have one, but ask permission first. Photocopy the original and scrapbook the copy, as ultrasound pictures fade with time. Don't photocopy it too many times, as the heat from the copier speeds up the fading process.

Congratulations!

For a wedding page, stick confetti around the edge, and save the place card which showed you where to sit for your meal. Many people decorate the meal table with all sorts of small shaped items which are ideal for scrapbook pages.

When You're Away

Holidays provide lots of memorabilia for your scrapbooking. Alongside holiday photos, include travel tickets, postcards, details of where you stayed, foreign money, and scraps of newspapers from the area.

Lazy Days

Your pages don't have to tell the story of grand events. You might have a great photo of you playing in the garden in *summer*. Make 'summer' your theme, and include some pretty pressed flowers (see page 35).

Embellishments

Many of the sample scrapbook pages you have seen include small items of decoration to finish the look of a page. Here's a quick run down of things you can use for your projects.

Holding it Together

Split pins (often called brads by scrapbookers) can be used to decorate the page, or to hold other items in place. To attach a photo to a piece of card, make holes in the corners of your photo with a hole punch. Then hold the card behind the photo, and push the closed brads through the holes. Separate and flatten the metal prongs on the reverse of the card, as shown (left) to hold the photo in place.

A Mixture of Materials

Use buttons to add small details, or to make a frame around a photo. Lace is great for wedding pages, or to give a nostalgic feel with old family photos. Buy metal inserts or use washers to add a cool, metallic look. Jewellery wire can be used almost like ribbon, twisted into shapes and letters with beads threaded on for decoration.

Flower Pressing

Collect your own flowers and press them by keeping them flat between two pieces of kitchen paper. Place a heavy book on top (above, inset) and leave for at least a week until they're dry. Your flowers will keep in your scrapbook without turning brown or looking past their best, although they may have lost some of their colour during the pressing process.

If you've been a bridesmaid and carried a bouquet, you can press the flowers in this way – or use the method to preserve daisy chains you've made with your friends. Flowers with a flat 'face', such as pansies, press best.

35

Family Fun

You will need:

- family photos
- metallic pen(s)
- glue
- scissors
- blue chalk
- a blue
- felt-tip pen
- net material
- silver string
- pink ribbon ● tin foil

Embellishments:

- self-adhesive stars
- sticky gems
- shop-bought decorations

You can make a page that features your whole family to show everyone how special you think they are, or just feature one person on each page.

Papers:

- light pink
- bright pink
- purple
- mid pink
- dark pink
- pale blue

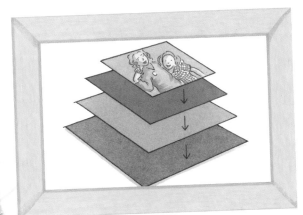

1 Mat a square photo, like this one of the two sisters, onto three layers of matting. Here we've used mid pink with a 15 mm border, bright pink with a 3 mm border, and purple with 10 mm showing. (See page 16 for instructions on matting photographs.)

2 Decorate the photo with a frame of self-adhesive stars. Add journalling using a metallic pen.

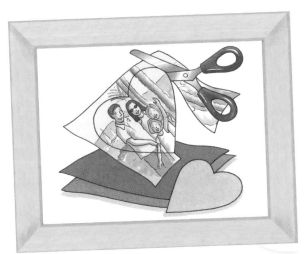

3 Use a heart template to draw around a family photo and carefully cut it out. Add two layers of matting in mid pink and purple, both with a 3 mm border.

4 Make another heart shape out of bright pink paper and mat it onto a larger purple heart. Add a shiny border and more journalling with your metallic pen. *Use this journalling to label who is in the main photo.*

Scrapattack Tip

If you haven't got a shop-bought heart template, make your own from a piece of strong card (or just use a cereal box). Trace a heart in a magazine to get the shape right.

5 Cut a strip of light pink paper, smudge the edge with chalk and decorate with stars. To make a tutu, cut four layers of tissue paper, and cut around them to create a tulip shape, as pictured. Glue the layers together at the bodice. Stick tiny criss-cross lengths of silver string to the bodice, then cut and glue pieces of net material to go over the skirt. Finish with ribbon stuck to the waist in a v-shape.

37

6 Cut a piece of light blue paper to fit exactly onto your scrapbook page, but don't stick it down yet. Add hand-drawn stars and more chalk (or ink) around the edges.

7 Glue the first photo, the pink strip, the two hearts, and the tutu in place. You could also cut a little tiara from tin foil for a tiara, and add it next to your tutu.

8 Add your shop-bought decorations and sticky stars, and fill up empty spaces with more journalling. Finally, stick your project into your scrapbook.

Scrapattack Tip
It can be hard to decide what to write in your journalling, so keep it simple. Why not ask family members to write their names on in their best handwriting?

MY SISTER IS A STAR ✦ MY SISTER IS A STAR ✦ MY SISTER IS A STAR ✦ MY SISTER IS A STAR ✦ MY SISTER IS A

Little Princess

DAD • MUM
SISTER • MUM • DAD
DAD • NIOMY • KE
KENDRA

A Cool Day Out

You will need:
- photos of your day out
- glue • scissors
- double-sided tape
- a black pen or pencil

Embellishments:
- Raffia or dried grass

Papers:
- light brown • yellowy-brown
- dark brown • black

Choose photos from your days out, and think carefully about how to lay them out and decorate them to fit the theme of the photos.

1 Cut a rectangle of light brown card that's a little bigger than one of your photos. Tear off a piece of yellowy-brown card and glue it to the bottom of the large piece. Trim the bottom and sides, then glue on your photo at an angle.

2 Cut a piece of dark brown card to the same height as your light brown matting. Tear it roughly in half. Wrap raffia or grass around the half you want to use, and fix it in place on the back using.the double-sided tape.

3 Peel off the second backing from the tape and stick the dark brown paper onto the light brown paper. Stick the whole thing in place onto a black paper background that's big enough to cover your scrapbook page.

Scrapattack Tip
Add tiny pinprick dots of white onto the black background using a white pencil. This adds a very subtle extra element to an otherwise plain background.

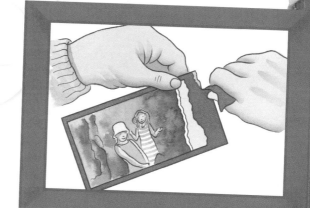

4 Tear down one edge of a smaller photo, making sure you don't tear into the picture of the people you want to feature. Matt the photo on light brown paper and cut it to fit, leaving one edge showing by the torn edge of the photo.

5 Matt the photo onto dark brown paper, leaving a wider border at the right-hand side. Tear this edge, too, then glue this photo onto your background.

6 Crop another photo to fit onto your background. Tear a small strip of dark brown paper to fit along one edge of the photo. With your fingers, gently roll up the uneven edges to give a 3-D effect (see page 13). Glue the rolled paper in place and stick the photo onto the background.

7 Add a title using small squares of yellowy-brown paper. Cut them and arrange them on the raffia to ensure that they fit in the space you have. Add hand-written letters and attach them using double-sided tape.

8 Add more journalling onto a torn, matted piece of card. Write words that express how you felt, or add details about the location and date of your visit. Finally, stick your completed project into your scrapbook.

Scrapattack Tip
Turn back to page 31 for a handy journalling tip if you're not very good at doing fancy lettering.

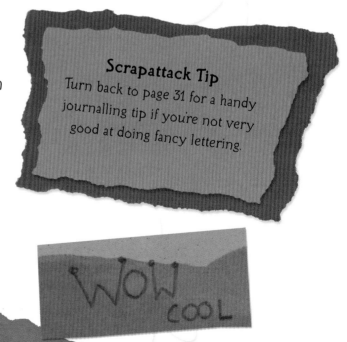

CAVES

WOW COOL

Pets Galore

Let your scrapbooking talents go wild with a page for one pet, or all the favourite animals in your home!

1 Cut a square piece of brown paper the right size to fit your scrapbook page. Don't stick it in just yet.

2 Tear strips of gold card to make a striped background. Glue them onto the brown card and trim off any overhang.

3 Add black paw prints to the gold strips with your black marker pen. Let them dry properly before you touch them to avoid smudging.

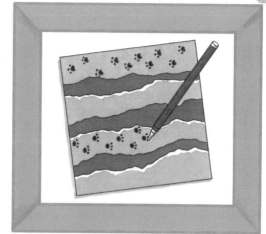

4 Crop your photos and then add matting to some or all of them using a mixture of black, cream and brown card. Vary the size of the borders depending upon the size of the photos. If you're unsure about matting photos with straight edges, turn back to page 16.

5 Experiment with the layout of the page. When you're happy with the layout, stick your photos in place. Cut rectangles of cream paper to label each photo.

CLIDE

Scrapattack Tip
Your journalling can be informative, giving each pet its name, or just fun, such as DO NOT FEED!

6 Add pet word stickers to suitable photos. Look in the shops for stickers with a clear background. You can add these to a photo so that the only thing that shows is the writing. Here, we've used MEOW! and PLAYTIME! on the kitten photo.

7 Use your bought letters or make your own to form a heading. Large, hand-drawn bubble letters, or stencilled capitals look good. Cut them out, and colour them in with animal prints.

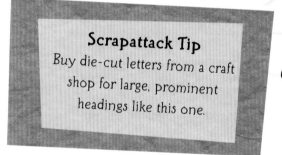

Scrapattack Tip
Buy die-cut letters from a craft shop for large, prominent headings like this one.

8 Attach the letters to the page using sticky foam pads to make them stand out and look 3-D. Now stick your finished project into your scrapbook.

MY PETS

MY HAM STER CAGE

DO NOT FEED

JEM

BONNY

CLIDE

playtime! meow

Fun In the Sun

Make a page for your favourite holiday snaps. This summer holiday page is light and airy to capture the mood of the photographs.

1 Cut the turquoise paper to fit your scrapbook page but don't glue it in place yet. Tear a strip of cream paper and glue it at the bottom of the page. Trim the edges to size.

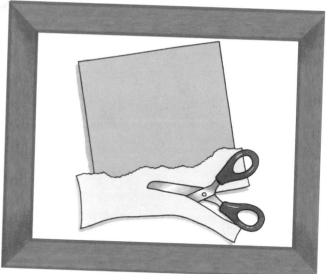

2 Decorate the 'sand' with your gold pen. Draw on small circles and spots to look like sand and stones.

48

3 Crop your photos and mount them onto pale blue matting. Tear small pieces of light brown paper to use as labels. Glue them in place on the photos.

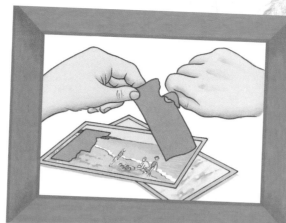

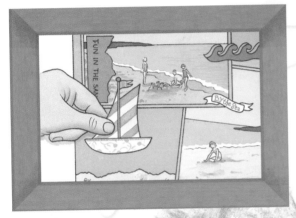

4 Arrange the photos in a suitable layout. Glue them in place and add self-adhesive embellishments (seaside shapes, starfish, waves and so on) to the whole page.

Scrapattack Tip

If you haven't got any gel pens, why not use real sand to create a beach effect? Rub a small amount of glue along the foot of your page using a glue stick, then shake your sand over the top. Leave to dry before shaking off any excess.

5 If you haven't got any sticker embellishments, make your own. Look for suitable pictures in magazines or on gift wrap. Cut them out, mount them on card, and stick them in place with foam pads to make them three-dimensional.

6 Add a label saying when and where the holiday snaps were taken. Fill in any gaps in the sea by drawing waves with your silver and blue gel pens.

7 Remember, one way to make your scrapbook personal and special is to keep mementoes from holidays and days out. Collect small shells and grains of sand and attach them to the corners of your page.
Finally, stick your project into your scrapbook.

Scrapattack Tip
Be careful when handling pages with delicate items on, like shells. Put these projects nearer to the top of your scrapbook so they don't get crushed.

FUN IN THE SAND

By the Sea

GREECE

JUNE 2005

School's Cool

It's great to look back on your schooldays and see how you looked on your first day, or for your first school photo in uniform! Try to capture what school felt like for you.

1 Cut the red paper to fit your scrapbook page but don't stick it in yet. Tear a piece of old homework to glue along the bottom edge of the red paper and cut it to size.

2 Tear a piece of black paper, roughly half the size of your page, and glue it along the left-hand edge.

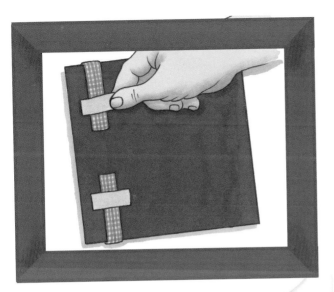

3 Cut a piece of ribbon that's about 5 cm longer than your page. *Use double-sided tape to attach it down the left-hand side, overlapping at the top and bottom edges and taping it on the back, too.*

4 Matt your school photo onto white paper, leaving a border of at least 3 mm. Place it on your page to get a feel for what space is left.

5 Make a rectangular 'blackboard' out of black paper. Matt it on brown paper.
Make sure the rectangle is the right shape and size to fit nicely on your page with your school photo. *Use a white pencil or gel pen to write on the blackboard.* This journalling is your own expression of however you feel about school. Use it to list your favourite things, your best subjects, or your exam results.

Scrapattack Tip
If you have scrapbooking chalk, add a few smudges to the edges of the blackboard for extra effect.

GOOD WORK

6 Cut a large gold star from your gold card and stick it on the page. Use black marker pen to write on it – maybe GOOD WORK or the date the photo was taken. Or, write the name of your school, if people who look at your scrapbook don't know which school you attend.

7 Finish the page by cutting out some foam letters to add a title down the side of your page, on top of the ribbon. If you like, you could buy ready-made die-cut letters instead.

8 Remember that personal items make great embellishments. Add your school badge or logo, or a prefect's badge. To finish, stick your project into your scrapbook.

WELL DONE
10/10

Scrapattack Tip
Choose different colours for your page to match your school's uniform.

A
B
C

I LIK

1. BECAUSE I CAN PLAY WITH MY FRIENDS

2. BECAUSE OF PACKED LUNCH

3. MY TEACHER

GOOD WORK

again. 10/10 WELL DONE

Baby Photos

You will need:
- a baby photo
- glue
- coloured marker pen
- double-sided tape

Embellishments:
- foam or die-cut letters
- fabric flowers
- buttons
- silver ribbon
- baby embellishments (like a duck sticker)

Hunt out your old baby photos and make a page that's devoted just to you! Many people who look at your scrapbook may never have seen you as a baby.

Papers:
- pastel coloured paper - 2 colours
- bright coloured paper - 2 colours
- bright pink

1 Cut a piece of pastel-coloured card (here, we've used pink) to fit your scrapbook page. but don't stick it in just yet. Cut another piece from a different pastel colour (here, yellow) and tear it in half before attaching it to the page.

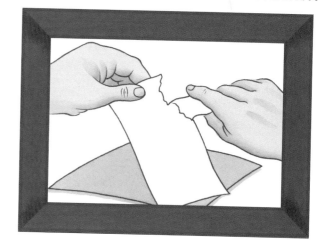

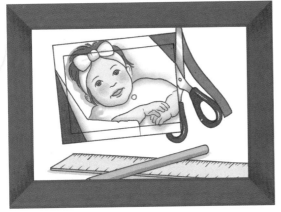

2 Crop your baby photo. If it's very precious and you don't want to spoil it, scan it in and print it out from a computer, or take a colour photocopy.

3 Cut a rectangle of bright card (here, bright pink) big enough to fit your photo with room for journalling underneath. Cut a similar sized piece of your second colour (here, purple) and tear it down the middle.

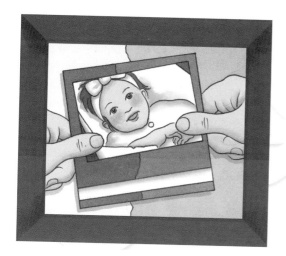

4 Glue the torn piece onto the complete rectangle, so that it looks like your matting is made from two halves of torn paper. Stick your photo in place at a slight angle. Attach a strip of silver ribbon across the bottom, then stick the whole thing at an angle on your page.

5 Cut a strip of bright pink paper to label your photo. Hand-write or print your text onto it and add a small flower for embellishment. Stick it in place down the side of the photo.

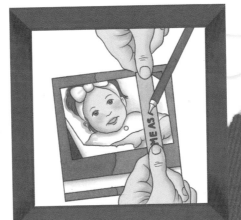

Scrapattack Tip
Use a pen and ruler to add fake stitching around the edge of your label. If you're feeling brave, use real stitching — it looks great! See page 21 for more hints on this.

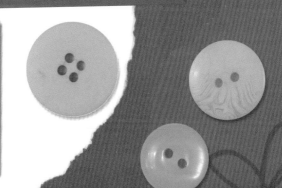

6 Spell out your name along the silver ribbon by cutting out the individual letters from bright pink paper or use foam letters. Try arranging them in a straight line, or slightly higgledy-piggledy. Decorate the letters with small fabric flowers.

7 Attach more fabric flowers along the top, and add a 3-D baby sticker at the bottom, like this cute yellow duck.

8 Stick buttons down the edge of your page using strong glue or foam pads as they will easily come loose otherwise. Finally, stick your project into your scrapbook.

Scrapattack Tip
Before you attach the buttons, try sewing through the holes. When they're stuck down, they'll look as if you've sewn them in place!

ME AS A BABY

KENDRA

Happy Birthday to Me!

You will need:

- a pretty paper clip
- glue and glue dots
- a photo of you at your party
- silver and purple gel pens

Embellishments:

- foam or cut-out letters
- alphabet/number stickers
- white fabric flowers
- foam flowers
- Happy Birthday cake decoration

Papers:

- purple
- light pink
- bright pink

You absolutely have to make a scrapbook page for your special day – the one day of the year where everybody is concentrating just on YOU!

1 Crop your photo and cut a square of bright pink paper to mount it on. Make sure the paper is at least 2 cm wider than the photo, and about 5 cm longer. Before you mount the photo, cut and tear purple and light pink strips of card to layer at the bottom.

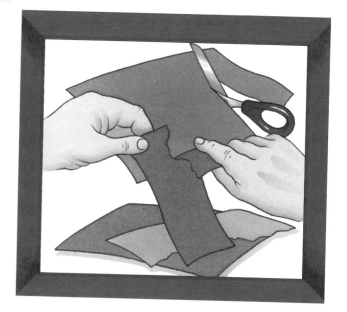

2 Glue all the layers of paper in place, and then mount the photo at an angle. Decorate the left-hand edge by sticking on a strip of small white fabric flowers.

3 Write a 'memory list' (all the cool things that happened at your party, and what presents you received) on a piece of white paper, then fold in half, as shown. Put to one side.

4 Cut a square of purple card to cover your scrapbook page. Don't stick it down just yet.

5 Cut a piece of light pink paper the same height as your page. Fold along the edge to make a small flap, then glue it to the back of your page (the free edge of the paper should overlap the right-hand side of your page when you turn it back over). Place the wish list under the flap, and cut just enough of the remaining paper to cover the list. Take the list out.

Scrapattack Tip
Visit a fabrics shop to find a massive selection of embroidered flowers in lots of styles and colours.

6 Carefully tear along the length of your light pink paper flap and put the wish list inside. Decorate the flap by writing 'Birthday List' in purple gel pen, then go over with silver gel pen once it has dried. Add a foam flower and use your paper clip to hold down the folded card.

Scrapattack Tip
You can use a pocket like this to hide secrets in your scrapbook. If you don't want people to read what's inside, don't write on the front and people won't know it's a special flap.

7 Now you can finish embellishing your page. Add the foam letters (or cut-outs), as shown to spell out your heading, BLOW. Use your silver gel pen to write 1,2,3... above your letters.

8 Use your stickers to show how old you were on that particular birthday (7 TODAY). Then ask an adult to cut the prongs from your cake decoration, and attach it with glue dots. Finally, stick your project into your scrapbook.

Glossary

Aged
Looking as though it has been around a long time – an effect achieved with chalk and crumpling.

Cropping
Cutting a photograph to change its shape or size.

Embellishments
Adding items, such as split pins, stickers, jewellery wire, string and ribbon to provide interest to the page.

Focal points
The areas on the page that draw the person's eye first, can be based around a grid layout.

Framing
Putting a cardboard edge over your picture to cover the edges. Frames can also be made from items such as string, buttons or lolly sticks.

Journalling
Adding words and numbers to a page, using a variety of materials, including pens, foam letters, cut-out card pieces and stickers.

Matting
Adding extra layers behind a picture to draw attention to it. Matts are often made from paper or card, but almost any material can be used.

Memorabilia
Collected items such as leaflets and tickets that remind you of the events in the photographs,

Landscape
A layout or photo for example, that is wider than it is high. **Portrait** is the opposite.

Layout
The way in which photos, backgrounds and embellishments are arranged on a page.

Theme
The 'story' behind a page, or the common link to all the photographs eg; a netball match, a holiday, or members of the same family or club.

Vellum
Semi-transparent paper, a bit like tracing paper but in different colours and patterns.